Grammar & Punctuation

Pupil Book **Year 2**

Shelley Welsh

Features of this book

- Clear explanations and worked examples for each grammar and punctuation topic from the KS1 National Curriculum.

- Questions split into three sections that become progressively more challenging:

Warm up

Test yourself

Challenge yourself

- 'How did you do?' checks at the end of each topic for self-evaluation.

- Regular progress tests to assess pupils' understanding and recap on their learning.

- Answers to every question in a pull-out section at the centre of the book.

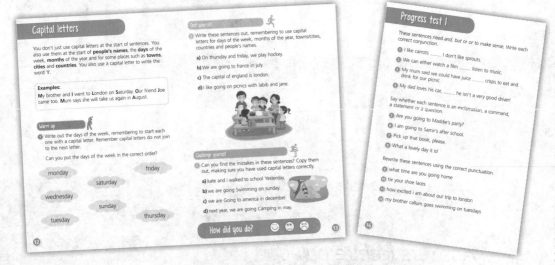

Contents

Writing sentences

A sentence always starts with a **capital letter** and often ends with a **full stop**.

A sentence needs to make complete sense – otherwise, it's not a sentence.

> **Example:**
>
> This is a sentence: *I jumped over the wall.* ✓
>
> This isn't a sentence: *over the wall* ✗

A sentence has a **verb**, which is a doing or being word. The verb in the example sentence above is **jumped**.

Warm up

1. Copy and complete the table, writing the groups of words below under the correct headings. Two examples have been done for you.

~~three little kittens~~   ~~We are playing cards.~~

Stella threw the ball.   high in the sky

a bright blue bird   They are eating fruit.

Sentences	Not sentences
We are playing cards.	three little kittens
Stell a tre threw high ther sky	
They are eating strina braght brau birl	

2 Read the text below out loud to yourself. Can you add capital letters and full stops so that it makes sense? Write the **four** sentences.

> my best friend is coming to my house tomorrow he always makes me laugh his name is Sam we go to the same school.

3 Make sentences from the jumbled-up words below and write them out. Remember to punctuate them correctly!

a) the   bush   scratched   my   arm   on   I

b) homework   we   on   our   did   Sunday

c) likes   our   puppy   on   the   rolling   grass

d) been   I   have   practising   spellings   my

e) ate   and   salad   for   we   lunch   pizza

How did you do?

Joining words and sentences with *and, but and or*

You can make two short sentences into one longer sentence by using the **conjunctions** (joining words) *and, but* and *or*. Having a mixture of short and long sentences makes your writing more interesting. Sometimes, you will need to make changes so that you aren't repeating words.

Examples:

Short sentences		One longer sentence
I like jelly.	I like ice-cream.	I like jelly **and** ice-cream.
Jack plays tennis.	Jack doesn't play cricket.	Jack plays tennis **but** he doesn't play cricket. (Instead of saying *Jack plays tennis but Jack doesn't play cricket*, you change the second 'Jack' to 'he'.)
Keisha doesn't eat chocolate.	Keisha doesn't eat crisps.	Keisha doesn't eat chocolate **or** crisps. (Using 'or' is better than saying, *Keisha doesn't eat chocolate and Keisha doesn't eat crisps*.)

Warm up

1) You need *and, but* or *or* in each of these sentences so that they make sense. Write each correct word.

a) Mum asked if I preferred juice _____ water with my lunch.

b) When I go swimming, I take my towel _____ my goggles.

c) I don't like learning spellings _____ I do like learning times tables!

d) We could choose to do either singing _____ dancing on the last day of term.

2 Find the **two** sentences in the passage that have used the wrong conjunction, and write them out using the correct word.

> I like apples or I don't like pears. My brother eats both fruit and vegetables. On Saturdays, Dad buys biscuits but ice-cream for a treat. They're yummy together; we like chocolate chip cookies with vanilla ice-cream best of all.

Challenge yourself

3 Make one longer sentence out of each pair of short sentences by joining them with a suitable conjunction. Don't copy any words that are not necessary.

a) We went to the seaside. We didn't go in the cold sea.

b) Our friends visited us this morning. They couldn't stay long.

c) In the café, Grandad didn't like the tea. Grandad didn't like the coffee.

d) In the afternoon, we played on the swings. We played on the slide.

How did you do?

Statements and questions

There are different types of sentences.

A **statement** is a sentence that tells you something. Like all sentences, it starts with a **capital letter**. A statement ends with a **full stop**.

Examples:

On Saturdays, we go swimming**.**

I like crisps but not nuts**.**

A **question** is a sentence that asks something. It starts with a **capital letter** and ends with a **question mark**.

Examples:

What time is your swimming lesson**?**

How are you**?**

Warm up

1 Decide whether each sentence is a statement or a question.

a) Are you ready for school?

b) There are 28 pupils in my class.

c) We are going to the park later.

d) Have you got my book?

2 Rewrite each sentence using the correct punctuation.

a) my dog likes chasing cats

b) which is your favourite subject

c) have you seen my pen

d) insects have six legs

3 Can you write **two** statements of your own? Use the pictures to help you.

a)

b)

4 Now write **two** questions of your own. Use the pictures to help you.

a)

b)

How did you do?

Exclamations and commands

An **exclamation** is a sentence where you show strong feelings like fear, anger, happiness or excitement. It starts with a **capital letter** and ends with an **exclamation mark**.

> **Examples:**
>
> **W**hat miserable weather it is**!**
>
> **H**ow tired I am**!**

A **command** is a sentence that tells you to do something. It starts with a **capital letter** and ends with either a **full stop** or an **exclamation mark**. It often starts with an **imperative verb**, which is a verb used to give a command.

> **Examples:**
>
> **Stir** the mixture slowly.   **Clean** up that mess now**!**

In the example sentences, **stir** and **clean** are **imperative** verbs.

Warm up

① Write out these command sentences, then underline the imperative verb in each one.

a) Put your shoes on.

b) Follow the leader.

c) Eat your breakfast.

d) Please tidy your room.

2 Decide whether these sentences are commands or exclamations.

a) Throw the ball.

b) What a big hairy spider that is!

c) Please drink your milk.

d) What massive teeth that shark has!

Challenge yourself

3 Write **two** exclamations. Use the pictures to help you.

a)

b)

4 Now write **two** commands. Use the pictures to help you.

a)

b)

Capital letters

You don't just use capital letters at the start of sentences. You also use them at the start of **people's names**, the **days** of the week, **months** of the year and for some places such as **towns**, **cities** and **countries**. You also use a capital letter to write the word '**I**'.

> **Examples:**
>
> **M**y brother and **I** went to **L**ondon on **S**aturday. **O**ur friend **J**oe came too. **M**um says she will take us again in **A**ugust.

Warm up

1 Write out the days of the week, remembering to start each one with a capital letter. Remember capital letters do not join to the next letter.

Can you put the days of the week in the correct order?

monday

friday

saturday

wednesday

sunday

tuesday

thursday

2 Write these sentences out, remembering to use capital letters for days of the week, months of the year, towns/cities, countries and people's names.

a) On thursday and friday, we play hockey.

b) We are going to france in july.

c) The capital of england is london.

d) I like going on picnics with labib and jane.

3 Can you find the mistakes in these sentences? Copy them out, making sure you have used capital letters correctly.

a) kate and i walked to school Yesterday.

b) we are going Swimming on sunday.

c) we are Going to america in december.

d) next year, we are going Camping in may.

How did you do?

Singular and plural nouns

A **noun** is a **naming word** for an object, person, animal, place, quality, characteristic or feeling. **Singular** means **one** of something, and **plural** means **more than one**. Usually, to make a noun plural you just add the letter **-s**.

Examples:

Singular	Plural
one girl	two girl**s**
that dog	those dog**s**
my coat	our coat**s**

Some nouns are a bit tricky to make plural. Look at these:

Examples:

Singular   **Plural**

For nouns ending in **x**, add **-es**.

this fox   these fox**es**

For some nouns ending in **f**, change the **f** to **v** and add **-es**.

one leaf   two lea**ves**

For nouns ending in a consonant followed by **y**, change the **y** to **i** and add **-es**.

her baby   their babi**es**

Warm up

1 Write the plural for each of these nouns.

a) flower   **b)** knee

c) donkey   **d)** spoon

2 To make the plural of these nouns, you need to change the **f** to **ves**. Write the correct plurals.

a) one thief ➔ *two...* **b)** the wolf ➔ *some...*

c) that shelf ➔ *those...* **d)** a loaf ➔ *a few...*

Challenge yourself

3 For each sentence, choose **two** nouns from the box below. Decide where they fit in the sentences and whether they should be singular or plural, then write out the **two** nouns.

berry	loaf	tree	box
leaf	baker	pencil	bush

a) The  fell off the .

b) Our teacher pointed out the red on the .

c) We filled the with .

d) Jamilla bought some fresh from the .

How did you do?

Progress test 1

These sentences need *and, but* or *or* to make sense. Write each correct conjunction.

1. I like carrots _____ I don't like sprouts.

2. We can either watch a film _____ listen to music.

3. My mum said we could have juice _____ crisps to eat and drink for our picnic.

4. My dad loves his car, _____ he isn't a very good driver!

Say whether each sentence is an exclamation, a command, a statement or a question.

5. Are you going to Maddie's party?

6. I am going to Samir's after school.

7. Pick up that book, please.

8. What a lovely day it is!

Rewrite these sentences using the correct punctuation.

9. what time are you going home

10. tie your shoe laces

11. how excited i am about our trip to london

12. my brother callum goes swimming on tuesdays

In these sentences, change the singular nouns in **bold** to the plural, and write them out.

13 Granny helped me lift the **box** onto the table.

14 We heard the **baby** crying.

15 I placed my books on the **shelf**.

16 My brother and I helped Dad sweep up the **leaf**.

17 Write your own statement.

18 Write your own exclamation.

19 Write your own question.

20 Write your own command.

Verbs – present tense

Verbs are usually **doing or being words**. They tell us what is happening in a sentence. We use the **present tense** when we are talking about something that is happening **now** or about an action that is **often repeated**.

There are two ways of writing the present tense.

Examples:

The clock **ticks**. (simple present) *or*
The clock **is ticking**. (progressive present)

I **run** for the bus. (simple present) *or*
I **am running** for the bus. (progressive present)

We **play** in the sand. (simple present) *or*
We **are playing** in the sand. (progressive present)

Warm up

1. Write out each present tense verb in the following sentences. To find the verb, ask yourself, "What is the person, or what are the people, doing?"

   a) Fred is watering the plants.

   b) Mattias swims every morning.

   c) Mum cooks dinner early on Saturdays.

   d) They are running on the beach.

2 The verbs in these sentences are in the progressive present tense. Write them in the simple present.

> **Example:** He is playing. ➜ *He plays.*

a) They are jumping.

b) Dad is cleaning.

c) Gran is knitting.

d) We are singing.

Challenge yourself

3 Write the missing present tense verb in each of the following sentences. Think about which form of the present tense makes most sense. (In one of these sentences, either form could be correct.)

a) We pictures today.

b) Every morning, Dan his teeth.

c) I usually  milk with my breakfast.

d) Erin the ball.

How did you do?

Verbs – past tense

We use the **past tense** when we are talking about something that has **already happened**.

There are two ways of writing the past tense.

> **Examples:**
>
> They **walked** the dog round the park. (simple past) *or*
>
> They **were walking** the dog round the park. (progressive past)

Warm up

1 Write out each past tense verb in the following sentences. To find the verb, ask yourself, "What was the person, or what were the people, doing?"

a) Amira jumped off the wall.

b) Jake and Molly were painting a picture.

c) Mrs Khan was washing her jumper.

d) They clapped at the end of the show.

e) We smiled at the little puppy.

f) I dried my wet hair.

2 The verbs in these sentences are in the progressive past tense. Write them in the simple past.

> **Example:** He was playing. → *He played*.

a) They were sighing.

b) I was dancing.

c) Raj was talking.

d) We were laughing.

Challenge yourself

3 Write the missing past tense verb in each of the following sentences. Think about which form of the past tense makes most sense. (For some of the sentences, either form could be correct.)

a) Brogan  in the pool.

b) On holiday, Finn lots of fish.

c) I in a tent with Dad when we went camping.

d) Monika in the playground.

How did you do?

Joining clauses with *when* and *if*

You can use the **conjunctions** *when* and *if* to **join** clauses to make longer sentences.

> **Examples:**
>
> I go to sleep **when** Mum turns off the light.
>
> I like playing outside **if** it is sunny.

You can also write *when* and *if* at the beginning of the sentence.

> **Examples:**
>
> **When** it is dark outside, we close the curtains.
>
> **If** my pencil is blunt, I sharpen it.

Warm up

1. These sentences need the conjunction *when* or *if* adding so they make sense. Choose the correct word and write it out. (In some of the sentences, either could be correct.)

   a) Aisha likes to drink water _____ she has her lunch.

   b) Tom said he would come in _____ it started raining.

   c) _____ it is sunny, we put sun cream on.

   d) _____ I eat too much chocolate, I feel a bit sick!

Answers

Pages 4–5

1. **Sentences:** Stella threw the ball. They are eating fruit.
   Not sentences: high in the sky; a bright blue bird
2. My best friend is coming to my house tomorrow. He always makes me laugh. His name is Sam. We go to the same school.
3. a) I scratched my arm on the bush.
   b) We did our homework on Sunday. *or:* On Sunday, we did our homework.
   c) Our puppy likes rolling on the grass.
   d) I have been practising my spellings.
   e) We ate pizza and salad for lunch. *or:* For lunch, we ate pizza and salad.

Pages 6–7

1. a) or
   b) and
   c) but
   d) or
2. I like apples but I don't like pears.
   On Saturdays, Dad buys biscuits and / or ice-cream for a treat.
3. a) We went to the seaside but we didn't go in the cold sea.
   b) Our friends visited us this morning but they couldn't stay long.
   c) In the café, Grandad didn't like the tea or the coffee.
   d) In the afternoon, we played on the swings and (on) the slide.

Pages 8–9

1. a) Question
   b) Statement
   c) Statement
   d) Question
2. a) My dog likes chasing cats.
   b) Which is your favourite subject?
   c) Have you seen my pen?
   d) Insects have six legs.
3. **Answers will vary. Examples:**
   a) Today it is raining.
   b) My cat drinks milk.
4. **Answers will vary. Examples:**
   a) What time is the next bus?
   b) Which cake would you like?

Pages 10–11

1. a) <u>Put</u> your shoes on.
   b) <u>Follow</u> the leader.
   c) <u>Eat</u> your breakfast.
   d) Please <u>tidy</u> your room.

2. a) Command
   b) Exclamation
   c) Command
   d) Exclamation
3. **Answers will vary. Examples:**
   a) How lovely my present is!
   b) What an amazing storm it is!
4. **Answers will vary. Examples:**
   a) Brush your teeth.
   b) Put the wrapper in the bin.

Pages 12–13

1. **Ensure that the initial capital letter has not been joined to the rest of the word and that the capital letter is approximately twice the height of the lower case letters without ascenders in each day. Check the days of the week are in the correct order.**
2. a) On Thursday and Friday, we play hockey.
   b) We are going to France in July.
   c) The capital of England is London.
   d) I like going on picnics with Labib and Jane.
3. a) Kate and I walked to school yesterday.
   b) We are going swimming on Sunday.
   c) We are going to America in December.
   d) Next year, we are going camping in May.

Pages 14–15

1. a) flowers
   b) knees
   c) donkeys
   d) spoons
2. a) two thieves
   b) some wolves
   c) those shelves
   d) a few loaves
3. a) leaves, tree
   b) berries, bush
   c) boxes, pencils
   d) loaves, baker

Pages 16–17

1. but
2. or
3. and
4. but
5. Question
6. Statement
7. Command
8. Exclamation
9. What time are you going home?
10. Tie your shoe laces.

1

Answers

11. How excited I am about our trip to London!
12. My brother Callum goes swimming on Tuesdays.
13. boxes
14. babies
15. shelves
16. leaves
17.–20. **Answers will vary. Ensure each sentence begins with a capital letter and ends with an appropriate final punctuation mark.**

Pages 18–19
1. a) is watering
   b) swims
   c) cooks
   d) are running
2. a) They jump.
   b) Dad cleans.
   c) Gran knits.
   d) We sing.
3. a) are drawing
   b) brushes
   c) drink
   d) is kicking / kicks

Pages 20–21
1. a) jumped
   b) were painting
   c) was washing
   d) clapped
   e) smiled
   f) dried
2. a) They sighed.
   b) I danced.
   c) Raj talked.
   d) We laughed.
3. a) was swimming / swam
   b) ate
   c) slept / was sleeping
   d) was skipping / skipped

Pages 22–23
1. a) when
   b) if / when
   c) When / If
   d) When / If
2. a) We all cheered when Yana scored a goal.
   b) Our teacher is annoyed when / if our homework is late.
   c) We all looked after Gran when she was ill.
   d) Sonny arrived late when the bus broke down.

3. **Answers will vary. Examples:**
   a) I put on my coat when it rains.
   b) Our teacher is cross if we make a mess.
   c) When it snows, we build a snowman.
   d) If I hurt myself, Dad looks after me.

Pages 24–25
1. a) because
   b) that
   c) because
   d) that
   e) that
2. a) Dad lit a fire because he needed to burn the leaves.
   b) I found my watch that I lost yesterday.
   c) My brother won a prize because he won the race.
   d) Lyla bought the game that she saw in the shop.
   e) Sheena watered the flowers that she planted last week.
3. **Answers will vary. Examples:**
   a) I like going to the park because there are lots of things to do.
   b) We put on our boots because it was raining.
   c) I know it was windy last night because the tree blew down in our garden.
   d) I felt very tired because I stayed up late.
   e) He went to a restaurant because he was hungry.

Pages 26–27
1. a) tasty
   b) new and red
   c) cheeky and little
   d) fluffy and warm
2. a) Silently, mysterious
   b) kindly, little
   c) carefully, hot
   d) excitedly, blue
3. **Answers will vary.**

Pages 28–29
1. a) our little red boat; the choppy sea
   b) the howling wind; the lashing rain
   c) the hot sunshine; the cold, frothy waves
   d) a silvery fish; the cool, clear water

2. **Answers may vary. The most likely example is:**
   First, we watched **the amazing dancers** in **their colourful, sparkly dresses**. Then, **some funny clowns** came into the ring. They wore **yellow, pointy hats** and **huge curly slippers**.
3. **Answers will vary.**

Pages 30–31
1. The dog **was running** on the beach.
2. Priya **was baking** a cake.
3. Mum **was cutting** the grass.
4. Joe **was counting** his money.
5. when
6. if
7. because / that
8. that
9. because
10. fierce, tired, beautiful
11. kind, muddy
12. roaring, hot
13. cautiously
14. Hungrily
15. magically
16. The shimmering blue butterfly; the pale pink flower
17. the fluttering snowflakes; the dark rooftops
18. Our playful little kitten; the steep stairs
19. is flying
20. is listening

Pages 32–33
1. a) verb
   b) adverb
   c) noun
   d) adjective
2. a) adverb
   b) adjective
   c) noun
   d) verb
3. **Answers will vary.**
4. **Answers will vary.**

Pages 34–35
1. a) Mum bought a pair of shoes, a hat, a bag and a coat.
   b) Our teacher handed out art books, pencils, paints and water.
   c) For my birthday, I got two footballs, a game, some sweets and lots of cards.
   d) We saw monkeys, snakes, elephants and giraffes at the zoo.

2. a) Mum, Dad, my brother and I went to the park.
   b) It was a snowy day so the swings, roundabout, seesaw and climbing frame were all white.
   c) We were glad we had wrapped up in warm coats, scarves, gloves and woolly hats.
   d) At home we had hot chocolate, toast and biscuits.

3. **Answers will vary.**

Pages 36–37
1. a) do not – don't
   b) there is – there's
   c) they have – they've
   d) I will – I'll
   e) could have – could've
   f) should not – shouldn't
   g) they are – they're
2. a) we've
   b) you're
   c) it's
   d) I'm
   e) they'll
3. a) can't
   b) There's
   c) she'd
   d) Don't
   e) We'd

Pages 38–39
1. a) brother's
   b) dog's
   c) sister's
   d) Mum's
   e) teacher's
2. a) the bird's wing
   b) my dad's hat
   c) my sister's scooter
   d) Jai's gloves
3. a) Niamh's
   b) grandfather's
   c) Mrs Smith's
   d) footballer's

Pages 40–41
1. a) Mum went to the shops to buy ice-cream, butter and milk.
   b) My sister went to London with her friend Henry.
   c) Have you seen my friend's dog?
   d) Tidy up that mess immediately.

Answers

2.   **a)**   clumsily, woolly
      b)   hot, carefully
      c)   old, slowly
      d)   quickly, angry
3.   Yesterday my dad's dog, Monty, chewed his slippers. Dad was cross with him, but Monty just rolled on his back and wagged his tail. Dad laughed and gave him a bowl of milk, a treat and a cuddle.

Pages 42–43
1.   Dan's
2.   friend's
3.   swimmer's
4.   dad's
5.   My mum packed my rucksack with my pyjamas, my slippers, my toothbrush and some toothpaste.
6.   After our meal, we had fruit, ice-cream, jelly and juice.
7.   The ingredients we needed were flour, sugar, butter and raisins.
8.   For my birthday, I got paints, pens, pencils and a drawing pad.
9.   we'd
10.   didn't
11.   I've
12.   couldn't
13.   shoe – noun
14.   eat – verb
15.   naughty – adjective
16.   noisily – adverb
17.   they had
18.   should not
19.   would have
20.   had not

2 Match the clauses, and then write them out to make sentences using *when* or *if*. (In one of the sentences, either could be correct.)

a) We all cheered	the bus broke down.
b) Our teacher is annoyed	she was ill.
c) We all looked after Gran	Yana scored a goal.
d) Sonny arrived late	our homework is late.

Challenge yourself

3 Write **four** of your own sentences using *when* and *if*. Use the pictures to help you.

a) I _____ when it _____.

b) Our teacher _____ if we _____.

c) When it _____, we _____.

d) If I _____, Dad _____.

How did you do?

Clauses starting with *that* and *because*

You can also use the words *that* and *because* to **introduce** a clause.

Examples:

Where are the books **that** I put on the table?

I like playing with Carla **because** she is fun.

We put on our coats **because** it began to rain.

I liked the cake **that** our teacher baked for us.

Warm up

1. These sentences need the word *because* or *that* adding so they make sense. Choose the correct word and write it out.

   a) Freddy drinks milk _____ it is healthy.

   b) Charlie found the pen _____ her brother had lost.

   c) We put on our hats _____ it was sunny.

   d) Where is the book _____ I was reading last night?

   e) I didn't like the ice-cream _____ we bought at the park.

2 Match the clauses, and then write them out as sentences using *because* or *that*.

a) Dad lit a fire   he won the race.

b) I found my watch   she saw in the shop.

c) My brother won a prize   he needed to burn the leaves.

d) Lyla bought the game   she planted last week.

e) Sheena watered the flowers   I lost yesterday.

3 Copy the clauses that end in *because*, and finish them yourself to make longer sentences.

a) I like going to the park because…

b) We put on our boots because…

c) I know it was windy last night because…

d) I felt very tired because…

e) He went to a restaurant because…

How did you do?

Adjectives and adverbs

Adjectives are words that **modify** nouns. 'Modify' means to add more detail to a word or words. Sometimes adjectives come before the noun, and sometimes they come after the verb *be*.

> **Examples:**
>
> My dad eats **smelly** cheese.
>
> ⇧ adjective ⇧ noun
>
> The flowers are **beautiful**.
>
> ⇧ noun ⇧ be ⇧ adjective

Adjectives can also describe feelings.

> **Examples:**   I feel **tired**.   Sam is **angry**.

Adverbs often give you **more information** about the verb (doing or being word) in a sentence. To find the adverb, find the verb then ask yourself, "*How* is the person doing what they are doing?"

> **Examples:**
>
> Ben ran **quickly** across the field. (How did Ben run?)
>
> **Angrily**, Sarah picked up her crayons. (How did Sarah pick up her crayons?)

 Warm up

① Find all the adjectives in these sentences and write them down.

    a) We ate all the tasty snacks.

    b) Our new car is red.

    c) I love my cheeky little puppy.

    d) Moyra put on her fluffy warm jumper.

2 Choose a suitable adverb and adjective to complete each of these sentences. Think about all of them before deciding. Then write out the complete sentences.

Adverbs:	silently	carefully	excitedly	kindly
Adjectives:	hot	mysterious	blue	little

a) _____ , we crept into the _____ cave.

b) Martha _____ helped her _____ brother to do his homework.

c) Mum _____ stirred the _____ soup.

d) Eva _____ put on her _____ dress for the party.

3 Write your own sentences containing these adjectives and adverbs.

a) colourful (adjective)

b) sparkling (adjective)

c) greedily (adverb)

d) quietly (adverb)

How did you do?

Expanded noun phrases

An **expanded noun phrase** gives the reader **more information** about a noun. You can do this by adding an adjective to modify the noun.

> **Example:**
>
> My little puppy has a short, curly tail.
>
> The expanded noun phrases are *my little puppy* and *a short, curly tail*.
>
> The first tells you more about the puppy and the second tells you more about its tail.

Warm up

1. Write out the **two** expanded noun phrases that you find in each of these sentences.

   a) Yesterday, we sailed our little red boat on the choppy sea.

   b) We were woken by the howling wind and the lashing rain.

   c) The hot sunshine warmed us after we splashed in the cold, frothy waves.

   d) I saw a silvery fish swimming in the cool, clear water.

2 Choose adjectives from the box below, then write out the passage so that it contains expanded noun phrases.

yellow	curly	colourful	amazing
sparkly	huge	pointy	funny

First, we watched **the** _____ **dancers** in **their** _____ , _____ **dresses**. Then, **some** _____ **clowns** came into the ring. They wore _____ , _____ **hats** and _____ _____ **slippers**.

3 Write your own sentences containing these expanded noun phrases.

a) the fluffy duckling

b) my bouncy ball

c) the huge scary giant

d) two friendly dinosaurs

How did you do?

Progress test 2

Write these progressive present tense sentences in the progressive past tense.

1. The dog **is running** on the beach.

2. Priya **is baking** a cake.

3. Mum **is cutting** the grass.

4. Joel **is counting** his money.

These sentences need the word *when* or *if* adding so they make sense. Write the correct word.

5. I always brush my teeth _____ I have had my breakfast.

6. My teacher said I could have a gold star _____ I learned my tables well.

These sentences need the word *because* or *that* adding so they make sense. Write the correct words.

7. Dad was cross _____ our puppy, Monty, had chewed his slippers.

8. They were his new ones _____ we had bought him for his birthday.

9. We think Monty chewed them _____ he was bored.

Write out all the adjectives in each of these sentences.

10 The fierce dragon felt tired as he chased the beautiful princess.

11 Our kind teacher cheered us as we ran round the muddy field.

12 We sat round the roaring fire and drank hot chocolate.

Write out the adverb in each of these sentences.

13 I opened my eyes then cautiously crept down the stairs.

14 Hungrily, Stella ate the delicious meal.

15 The magician magically produced a rabbit from his hat.

Write out the **two** expanded noun phrases in each of these sentences.

16 The shimmering blue butterfly landed on the pale pink flower.

17 We watched the fluttering snowflakes landing on the dark rooftops.

18 Our playful little kitten bounded up the steep stairs.

Write these progressive past tense sentences in the progressive present tense.

19 Luke **was flying** his kite.

20 Our class **was listening** to a talk about the Tudors.

Score ⬤/ 20

Word classes

You can **group** words according to their type or **class**.

Examples:

Nouns are naming words for objects, people, animals or places.

> The **man** walked his **dog** in the **park**.

Adjectives are words which modify nouns.

> The **beautiful** butterfly fluttered in the **blue** sky.

Verbs are doing or being words.

> I **am** happy when I **walk** to school.

Adverbs often give more information about the verb. They often end in **-ly**.

> Erin laughed **loudly**, then ran **quickly** into the garden.

Warm up

1. Decide whether each word in **bold** in these sentences is a noun, adjective, adverb or verb, and write out the word and the word class.

   a) My mum **stirred** the cake mixture.

   b) She poured it **carefully** into the tin.

   c) Then she put it in the **oven**.

   d) It tasted **delicious**!

2 Match each word to its word class, and write them out together.

a) swiftly   adjective

b) soft   verb

c) cloud   adverb

d) wear   noun

Challenge yourself

3 Write **two** sentences, both containing a verb and an adverb. Use these words to help you.

Verbs   **Adverbs**

| run walk eat cut | quickly slowly hungrily carefully |

4 Write another **two** sentences, this time both containing a noun and an adjective. Use these words to help you.

Nouns   **Adjectives**

| dog sun beach sea | scruffy sunny sandy shimmering |

How did you do?

Commas in lists

Commas separate groups of words within a sentence to help you make sense of it. You can use commas when you are writing a **list** of things.

Examples:

Mia and I bought some apples, bananas, cherries and pears.

Dev has pencils, a ruler, a sharpener and a pen in his pencil case.

In lists like these, you don't write a comma before the word *and*.

Warm up

1 Write out these sentences, inserting the missing commas.

a) Mum bought a pair of shoes a hat a bag and a coat.

b) Our teacher handed out art books pencils paints and water.

c) For my birthday, I got two footballs a game some sweets and lots of cards.

d) We saw monkeys snakes elephants and giraffes at the zoo.

2 The commas in these sentences are in the wrong places or are missing. Write the sentences out, putting the commas in the correct places.

a) Mum Dad my, brother and I went to the park.

b) It was a snowy day so the, swings roundabout seesaw and, climbing, frame were all white.

c) We were glad we had wrapped up in warm, coats scarves gloves and woolly, hats.

d) At home we had hot, chocolate toast, and biscuits.

Challenge yourself

3 Write a list of at least **three** things you would take if you went…

a) swimming

I would take…

b) on a picnic

I would take…

c) on holiday

I would take…

How did you do?

Apostrophes to make words shorter

You can sometimes make two words into one shorter word by taking away a letter or letters. You need to put the **apostrophe** just above where the **missing letters** would be.

Examples:

I am hungry.　　→　　I'm hungry.

We are cold.　　→　　We're cold.

The dog is barking.　　→　　The dog's barking.

Warm up

1 Match the words on the left with their shortened form on the right, and write them down together.

a) do not	I'll
b) there is	don't
c) they have	there's
d) I will	they've
e) could have	shouldn't
f) should not	they're
g) they are	could've

2 Use an apostrophe to turn each pair of words into one word, and write it out.

a) we have

b) you are

c) it is

d) I am

e) they will

Challenge yourself

3 The apostrophes have been put in the wrong place in each of the words in **bold** in these sentences. Write out the words correctly.

a) We **cant'** come to your party.

b) **Ther'es** a fly in my soup!

c) My auntie said **shed'** take me shopping.

d) **Do'nt** do that – it's really annoying.

e) **W'ed** better hurry up!

How did you do?

Apostrophes to show possession

You can show that something **belongs** to someone by using an **apostrophe**. The apostrophe goes between the last letter of the word and the letter **s**.

Examples:

The dog**'s** collar is too tight. (The collar belongs to the dog.)

We love my auntie**'s** baby! (The baby belongs to my auntie.)

Warm up

1 Decide where to insert an apostrophe in each of the words in **bold**, and write out the correct word.

a) My **brothers** hockey match was cancelled.

b) My **dogs** fur is brown.

c) My **sisters** coat is on the peg.

d) **Mums** favourite flowers are roses.

e) Our **teachers** computer is broken.

2 Write out these phrases so that they use an apostrophe to show that something belongs to someone.

> **Example:**
>
> the ball belonging to Kate ➔ *Kate's ball*

a) the wing belonging to the bird

b) the hat belonging to my dad

c) the scooter belonging to my sister

d) the gloves belonging to Jai

Challenge yourself

3 Pick the correct noun to fit into each sentence, then write the noun putting an apostrophe in the right place.

footballer	Mrs Smith	Niamh	grandfather

a) My friend _____ scarf was on the floor.

b) My _____ chair is very comfortable.

c) _____ car has broken down.

d) Everyone cheered the _____ goal.

Checking your work

After you have done your writing, remember to read back over your work. Ask yourself:

- Do my sentences make sense?
- Have I used the correct verb tense?
- Have I used adjectives and adverbs to add more detail?
- Is my punctuation correct?
- Is my spelling correct?

Example:

the cat was lie on the grass

What is wrong with this sentence? The verb tense (past progressive) has not been properly written. You can correct it *and* add more detail!

The ginger cat with the long whiskers was lying lazily on the green grass.

Warm up

1 Find the punctuation errors in these sentences and write them out correctly.

a) mum went to the shops to buy ice-cream butter and milk

b) my sister went to london with her friend henry

c) have you seen my friends dog

d) tidy up that mess immediately

2 These sentences can be made more detailed by adding adjectives and adverbs from the box below. Write out the more detailed sentences.

| old   carefully   clumsily   hot   quickly   woolly   angry   slowly |

a) I _____ ripped my new _____ jumper.

b) Our _____ soup was placed _____ on the table.

c) My grandad's _____ car crawled _____ up the road.

d) The thief ran _____ away from the _____ policeman.

3 Rewrite this passage, making sure each sentence makes sense and is correctly punctuated.

| yesterday my dads dog, monty, chews his slippers dad was been cross with him but monty just rolled on his back and wags his tail dad is laughing and gived him a bowl of milk a treat and a cuddle |

How did you do?

For each word in **bold**, decide where to put an apostrophe to show possession, then write the word correctly.

1. **Dans** new cricket bat is amazing.

2. My **friends** house was flooded in the storm.

3. That **swimmers** goggles are on the bottom of the pool.

4. Our **dads** bike has a flat tyre.

Write these sentences out, inserting the missing commas.

5. My mum packed my rucksack with my pyjamas my slippers my toothbrush and some toothpaste.

6. After our meal, we had fruit ice-cream jelly and juice.

7. The ingredients we needed were flour sugar butter and raisins.

8. For my birthday, I got paints pens pencils and a drawing pad.

Using an apostrophe, write the shortened form of these words.

9 we had

10 did not

11 I have

12 could not

Match each word on the left to its word class on the right and write them out together.

13 shoe   adverb

14 eat   noun

15 naughty   verb

16 noisily   adjective

Write these shortened words in their full form.

17 they'd

18 shouldn't

19 would've

20 hadn't

Published by Keen Kite Books
An imprint of HarperCollins*Publishers* Ltd
The News Building
1 London Bridge Street
London SE1 9GF

ISBN 9780008184513

First published in 2016

10 9 8 7 6 5 4 3 2 1

Text and design © 2016 Keen Kite Books, an imprint of HarperCollins*Publishers* Ltd

Author: Shelley Welsh

The author asserts her moral right to be identified as the author of this work.

Series Concept and Commissioning: Michelle I'Anson
Series Editor and Development: Shelley Teasdale & Fiona Watson
Inside Concept Design: Paul Oates
Project Manager: Rebecca Adlard
Cover Design: Anthony Godber
Text Design and Layout: Q2A Media
Production: Lyndsey Rogers
Printed in the UK

A CIP record of this book is available from the British Library.

Images are ©Shutterstock.com